SOUNDS LIKE READING
BOOK SIX

Whose Shoes Would You Choose?

A LONG VOWEL SOUNDS BOOK WITH CONSONANT DIGRAPHS

Brian P. Cleary

illustrations by

Jason Miskimins

Consultant:
Alice M. Maday

Ph.D. in Early Childhood Education with a Focus in Literacy
Assistant Professor, Retired
Department of Curriculum and Instruction
University of Minnesota

Ⓜ Millbrook Press/Minneapolis

to Miss Mac Ivor,
my fifth-grade teacher in Rocky River, Ohio
—B.P.C.

Text copyright © 2009 by Brian P. Cleary
Illustrations copyright © 2009 by Lerner Publishing Group, Inc.

Millbrook Press
A division of Lerner Publishing Group, Inc.
241 First Avenue North
Minneapolis, MN 55401 USA

For reading levels and more information, look up this title at www.lernerbooks.com.

Library of Congress Cataloging-in-Publication Data

Cleary, Brian P., 1959–
    Whose shoes would you choose? : a long vowel sounds book with
consonant digraphs / by Brian P. Cleary ; illustrations by Jason Miskimins ;
consultant: Alice M. Maday.
        p.   cm. — (Sounds like reading)
    ISBN 978–0–8225–7640–2 (lib. bdg. : alk. paper)
    ISBN 978–0–7613–5199–3 (eb pdf)
    1. English language—Consonants—Juvenile literature. 2. English
language—Vowels—Juvenile literature. 3. Reading—Phonetic method—
Juvenile literature. I. Miskimins, Jason, ill. II. Maday, Alice M. III. Title.
PE1159.C53 2009
428.1'3—dc22   2008012767

Manufactured in the United States of America
4-42991-8564-6/20/2022

Dear Parents and Educators,

As a former adult literacy coach and the father of three children, I know that learning to read isn't always easy. That's why I developed **Sounds Like Reading**®—a series that uses a combination of devices to help children learn to read.

This book is the sixth in the **Sounds Like Reading**® series. It uses rhyme, repetition, illustration, and phonics to introduce young readers to long vowel sounds and consonant digraphs—letter combinations that come together to create a new sound. These include combinations such as *ch*, *sh*, and *th*. I've chosen to use a broad, inclusive definition of digraphs in this book, so you'll also see combinations such as *kn* and *wr*.

Starting on page 4, you'll see three rhyming words on each left-hand page. These words are part of the sentence on the facing page. They all feature long vowels and consonant digraphs. As the book progresses, the sentences become more challenging. These sentences contain a "discovery" word—an extra rhyming word in addition to those that appear on the left. The final sentence in the book contains two discovery words. Children will delight in the increased confidence that finding and decoding these words will bring. They'll also enjoy looking for the mouse that appears throughout the book. The mouse asks readers to look for words that sound alike.

The bridge to literacy is one of the most important we will ever cross. It is my hope that the **Sounds Like Reading**® series will help young readers to hop, gallop, and skip from one side to the other!

Sincerely,

Brian P. Cleary

Brian P. Cleary

Look for me to help you find the words that sound alike!

shone

throne

phone

Can you find three words that sound alike?

The sun **shone** on the **throne** as he talked on the **phone**.

each

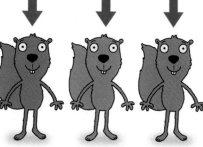

reach

peach

6

We **each reach** for a **peach**.

she

three

3

knee

She drew a **three** on her **knee**.

teach

speech

beach

He can **teach** the **speech** at the **beach**.

leech

bleach

screech

EEE!

Can you find three words that sound alike?

The **leech** by the **bleach**
made me **screech**.

whose

shoes

choose

Whose shoes should she **choose**?

chief

thief

sheaf

Can you find three words that sound alike?

The **chief** saw the **thief**
with the **sheaf**.

sheik

shriek

EEE!

cheek

EEE!

Can you find three words that sound alike?

18

The **sheik** will **shriek** if you kiss his **cheek**.

cheese

knees

wheeze

WHEEZE!

Can you find three words that sound alike?

The **cheese** on my **knees** made me **wheeze**.

Mr. Cho

know

throw

Show Mr. Cho that you **know** how to **throw**.

Keith

wreath

teeth

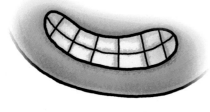

Can you find the word that sounds like Keith, wreath, and teeth?

Keith had a **wreath beneath** his **teeth**.

chew

shoe

threw

Can you find the word that sounds like chew, shoe, and threw?

She **knew** she should not **chew**
on the **shoe** that he **threw**.

chose

shows

knows

She **chose those shows** that her friend **knows**.

Ruth

tooth

booth

Can you find two words that sound like Ruth, tooth, and booth?

It is the **truth** that a **youth** named **Ruth** put a **tooth** in the **booth**.

Brian P. Cleary is the author of the best-selling Words Are CATegorical® series as well as the Math Is CATegorical®, Adventures in Memory™, Poetry Adventures, and Food Is CATegorical™ series. He has also written several picture books and poetry books. In addition to his work as a children's author and humorist, Mr. Cleary has been a tutor in an adult literacy program. He lives in Cleveland, Ohio.

Jason Miskimins grew up in Cincinnati, Ohio, and graduated from the Columbus College of Art & Design in 2003. He currently lives in North Olmsted, Ohio, where he works as an illustrator of books and greeting cards.

Alice M. Maday has a master's degree in early childhood education from Butler University in Indianapolis, Indiana, and a Ph.D. in early childhood education, with a focus in literacy, from the University of Minnesota in Minneapolis. Dr. Maday has taught at the college level as well as in elementary schools and preschools throughout the country. In addition, she has served as an emergent literacy educator for kindergarten and first-grade students in Germany for the U.S. Department of Defense. Her research interests include the kindergarten curriculum, emergent literacy, parent and teacher expectations, and the place of preschool in the reading readiness process.

For even more phonics fun, check out all eight SOUNDS LIKE READING® titles listed on the back of this book!

And find activities, games, and more at www.brianpcleary.com.

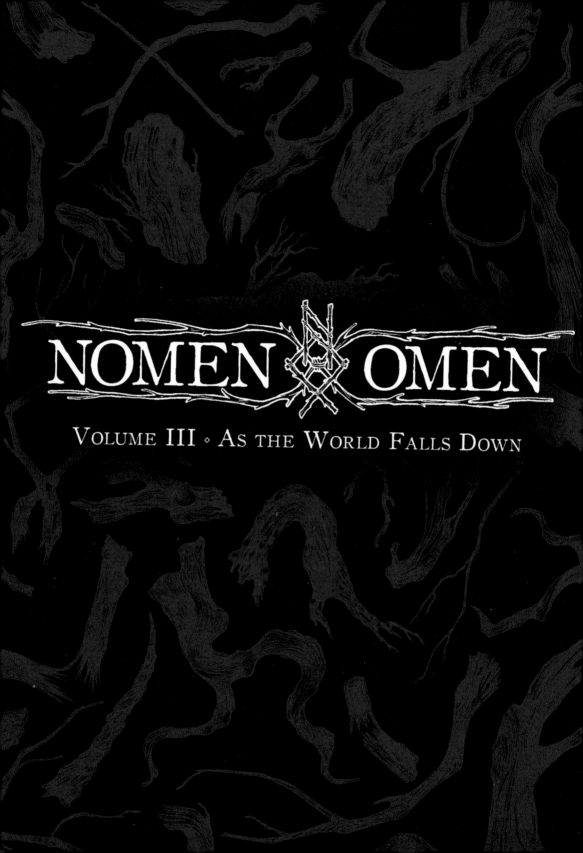

NOMEN ✦ OMEN

VOLUME III ◦ AS THE WORLD FALLS DOWN

NOMEN OMEN

WRITER
MARCO B. BUCCI

ARTIST AND COLORIST
JACOPO CAMAGNI

◆

EDITORS
DIEGO MALARA
AND STEFANIA SIMONINI

LETTERING
FABIO AMELIA (ARANCIA STUDIO)

◆

TRANSLATION FROM ITALIAN
ARANCIA STUDIO

DREAM SEQUENCES PAINTED BY
FABIO MANCINI

ADDITIONAL COLORS
FABIOLA IENNE

DESIGN
ALESSANDRO GUCCIARDO
AND FABIO AMELIA

COVER ARTWORK BY JACOPO CAMAGNI

NOMEN OMEN, VOL. 3: AS THE WORLD FALLS DOWN. First printing. June 2021. Published by Image Comics, Inc. Office of publication: PO BOX 14457, Portland, OR 97293. Copyright © 2021 Marco B. Bucci and Jacopo Camagni. All rights reserved. Contains material originally published in single magazine form as NOMEN OMEN #11-15. "Nomen Omen," its logos, and the likenesses of all characters herein are trademarks of Marco B. Bucci and Jacopo Camagni, unless otherwise noted. "Image" and the Image Comics logos are registered trademarks of Image Comics, Inc. No part of this publication may be reproduced or transmitted, in any form or by any means (except for short excerpts for journalistic or review purposes), without the express written permission of Marco B. Bucci and Jacopo Camagni, or Image Comics, Inc. All names, characters, events, and locales in this publication are entirely fictional. Any resemblance to actual persons (living or dead), events, or places, without satirical intent, is coincidental. Printed in the USA. ISBN: 978-1-5343-1907-3.

NOMEN OMEN is a PANINI COMICS Italy original production. CEO: Aldo H Sallustro, Publishing and Licensing Director: Marco M. Lupoi,

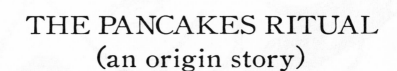

THE PANCAKES RITUAL
(an origin story)

In the fall of 2008, I flew for the first time to New York, destination Comicon, for the celebration of the winners of the Chester Quest, the competition organized by Marvel Comics to find new talented artists, which marked the beginning of my career as an overseas artist...

Obviously, I was very excited because soon I was going to start working on comics for a big publisher. Legs trembled at the fulfillment of a dream.

During the first day of the fair, I finally had the opportunity to meet Becky Cloonan in person, the author who, together with Bruce Timm and Jamie Hewlett, contributed significantly to my passion, to the definition of my style, to the growth of my imagination.

We had known each other virtually for some time through the Deviantart website, the virtual place where designers at the time exhibited their works. I loved her gothic imagery populated by female figures (who all looked like witches), wolves, knights, and fantastic creatures. I loved her stroke, those dirty and dark signs that combined with original and refined designs.

I was excited at the idea of meeting her face to face, she was already working for the big names in the industry and I was looking shyly at my American path. I remember that we had made an appointment at the entrance to the fair. Becky was exactly as I had imagined her: nice, very rock.

We decided to go for lunch together to tell each other about our lives in a quiet place. It was the Skylight Diner, which she knew and which was to become the place where this whole story began. I still did not know, but later the memories and the atmosphere of that day would be the vital spark for the saga you are reading.

Nomen Omen was born in Manhattan, a few nights after that meeting, when Bucci and I found ourselves fantasizing together about a fantasy story set all around us. It was inevitable. We were out and about in that familiar city we were visiting for the first time. A false memory that fed on all the films and series that had shown it to us countless times since our childhood. We were full of that creative energy that only fair days can give, it was as if each location revealed the whole course of events as we visited them.

And it was absolutely natural, like reading a book. Except that the text was made up of intersections and various people, buildings and parks. What better place to tell a story about Incarnate Stories than Manhattan? It was and still remains the metropolis where people from all over the world converge, with their load of stories, traditions, hopes, and fantasies. I remember feeling carried away as if I could perceive this flow of different lives ready to meet and mingle. As if Manhattan itself was an entity unto itself, alive and familiar. After all, it lives in our imagination, who can say they don't know it at all?

The ideas came like a sudden tide, unable to stop, ready to permeate every memory. History almost wrote itself. It must have been the meeting with Becky or the pancakes at Skylight Diner. The thrill of Comicon or the colors of Central Park with its ravenous robins. Or the smell of the subway, the codes hidden in the graffiti, or the temple of Dendur at the Metropolitan Museum. The puddles that reflected the lights of Broadway or the Chinese herb shops... I really can't list all the ingredients of that spell. I only know that something has taken possession of me and Marco, and has asked us in a loud voice to give it life on paper, to tell the story of our Becky and that of an imaginary Manhattan dangerously similar to the real one.

Today, after so many years, every time I go back to New York, I can't help but stop by that diner, to order a giant portion of pancakes like that first time. Although now, to be honest, I am careful not to enter the toilet. I care too much about my heart. ;)

Jacopo Camagni
Rome, April 2021

Chapter 11

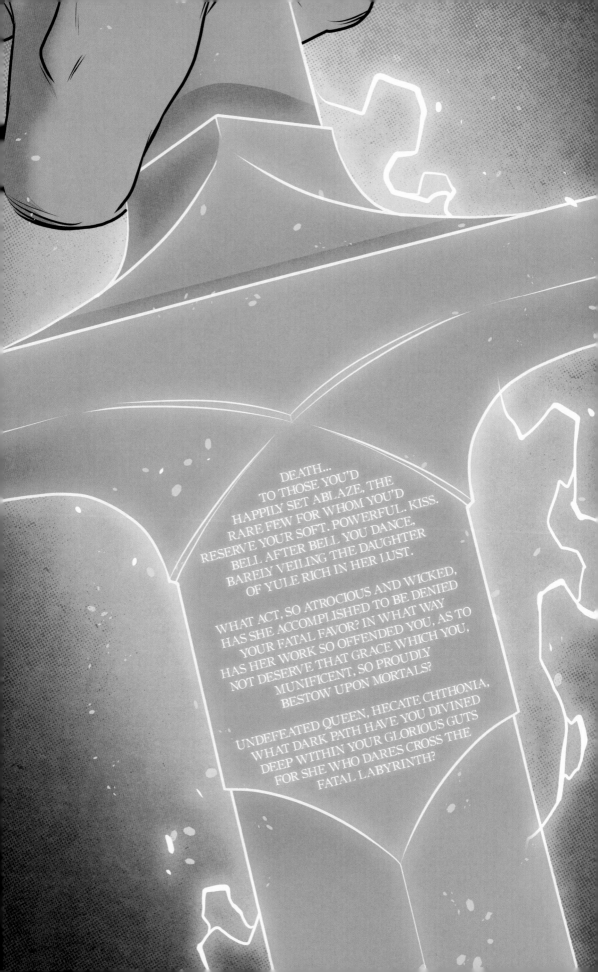

DEATH...
TO THOSE YOU'D
HAPPILY SET ABLAZE, THE
RARE FEW FOR WHOM YOU'D
RESERVE YOUR SOFT, POWERFUL, KISS.
BELL AFTER BELL YOU DANCE,
BARELY VEILING THE DAUGHTER
OF YULE RICH IN HER LUST.

WHAT ACT, SO ATROCIOUS AND WICKED,
HAS SHE ACCOMPLISHED TO BE DENIED
YOUR FATAL FAVOR? IN WHAT WAY
HAS HER WORK SO OFFENDED YOU, AS TO
NOT DESERVE THAT GRACE WHICH YOU,
MUNIFICENT, SO PROUDLY
BESTOW UPON MORTALS?

UNDEFEATED QUEEN, HECATE CHTHONIA,
WHAT DARK PATH HAVE YOU DIVINED
DEEP WITHIN YOUR GLORIOUS GUTS
FOR SHE WHO DARES CROSS THE
FATAL LABYRINTH?

GREENWICH VILLAGE.

THANK YOU *ALL* FOR COMING TO OUR SPECIAL LITTLE *NIGHT* PARTY. IT'S BECOME SOMETHING OF A *TRADITION*...

JUST AS *EVERY YEAR* WE GATHER TO CELEBRATE HALLOWEEN IN HONOR OF ALL THE *WOMEN* WHO'VE BEEN *PERSECUTED* FOR THEIR OWN UNIQUE NATURE.

BUT I THINK IT'S TIME I GAVE THE FLOOR TO *HELENA*, WHO'S HERE TONIGHT TO PRESENT HER NEW BOOK, *QUEER WITCHES*.

IT'S BEEN A *WHILE* SINCE WE'VE SEEN EACH OTHER...

BUT HOW COULD I MISS THIS? I MEAN...WHAT *HARM* COULD COME FROM LEAVING THE *CLINIC* FOR *ONE* NIGHT?

...AND *BECKY?*

TOO SMART. TOO GOOD, AS *USUAL*...AND *ALWAYS* WITH HER MIND *SOMEWHERE ELSE*. SHE'S *EXACTLY* LIKE CLAIRE...

WILL SHE JOIN US AT SOME POINT?

SURE, SHE CARES A LOT.

WHO COULD *BLAME* HER... THE PLACE IS *PACKED!*

THANKS TO MY *PUNCH.*

QUEER PEOPLE REJECT THE VERY IDEA OF PARADIGMS, REBELLING AGAINST THE CATEGORIES SOCIETY HOPES TO IMPOSE UPON THEM. THEY SHAPE THEIR IDENTITIES THROUGH SELF-DETERMINATION AND THE LANGUAGE THEY CHOOSE TO USE.

MANY OF THE WOMEN ONCE CALLED *"WITCHES"* WERE NOT SO DIFFERENT. THEY WERE PERSECUTED BECAUSE THEY REBELLED AGAINST THE ROLES THAT BOTH THE PATRIARCHY AND RELIGION WANTED TO IMPOSE ON THEM.

READING ABOUT THESE EXTRAORDINARY WOMEN, WE HAVE LONG HAD THE IDEA THAT THEIR DIFFERENCE WAS NOTHING MORE A REASON FOR SHAME AND FEAR, SOMETHING THAT FORCED THEM TO HIDE OR PRETEND TO BE THE SAME AS THEIR NEIGHBORS...

BUT HAS IT ALWAYS BEEN LIKE THIS? OR COULD IT BE THAT THIS IS NOTHING MORE THAN A WATERED-DOWN IDEA THAT HAS TAKEN CENTURIES TO REACH US? IN THIS BOOK, I HONOR THE LIVES OF WOMEN WHO WERE RESTLESS, NEVER SATISFIED TO STAY IN THEIR PLACE AND UNABLE TO KEEP THEIR MOUTHS SHUT.

THEY ACTIVELY LIVED THEIR INDIVIDUALITY OUTSIDE THE HERD. SOME OF THEM MANAGED TO CHANGE THEIR WORLD...

OTHERS WERE PERSECUTED, OTHERS KILLED. BUT NONE OF THE WOMEN I SPEAK OF EVER STOPPED BEING THEMSELVES. MY WORK HERE IS DEDICATED TO THEM...

WE'VE BEEN GOING ON LIKE THIS FOR *MONTHS...*

...AND I FEEL LIKE THE MOST MESSED UP GIRL...AND THE *LUCKIEST* GIRL IN THE WORLD.

BUT YOU'VE *GOT* TO JUST GET IT OVER WITH. YOU'RE NOT *JUST* IN A RELATIONSHIP WITH ME. THERE'S *SOMETHING* BETWEEN YOU TWO.

HAVEN'T YOU FIGURED IT OUT YET?!

FUCK IT...I HAVE TO START MY MAKEUP *OVER* FROM SCRATCH.

SLAM

SHE *JUST* TOLD US THAT...

YUP.

PAT

LOOK, YOU *DON'T* HAVE TO--

SHUT UP, DWARF.

CHELSEA.

DHARA SENT ME A MESSAGE. SHE'S *LATE*.

LIKE *SOPHIE*.

YOU *DO* LOOK *JUST* LIKE *NEMESIS* THOUGH!

THIS STUFF ITCHES LIKE HELL... IS IT REALLY NECESSARY?

IT'S A *COSTUME* PARTY. *NORMIES* AREN'T ALLOWED.

BY THE WAY, YOU'VE BEEN LOOKING... *STRANGE*... FOR A WHILE.

YOU SURE EVERYTHING'S *OKAY?*

HOW MANY *MORE* WAYS DO I HAVE TO *TELL* YOU *I'M FINE?* I MISS *PATRICK*. AND DHARA'S BEEN A BIT *DISTANT*.

OTHERWISE...

HERE, LET'S SEE WHERE THAT *FOOL* IS...

ANYWAY...YOU *KNOW* YOU CAN TELL ME *ANYTHING*, RIGHT?

LOOK... YOU'RE THE *STRANGE* ONE. YOU ASK ME THESE *ABSURD* QUESTIONS, YOU *KILL* YOURSELF WITH *STRESS*, I CATCH YOU *SNEAKING* AROUND ALL THE TIME...

...*YOU'RE* THE ONE THAT LOOKS LIKE HE'S BEEN *HIDING* SOMETHING.

BECKY, I...

TLACK

HERE I *AM!* BADASS ZOMBIE SLAYER REPORTING!

WHERE'S MY FAVORITE MONSTER...?

...AND *AGAIN* WITH THE AWKWARD SILENCES.

I HEARD FROM DHARA, THEY'RE WAITING FOR US AT THE *SKYLIGHT* TO HAVE A DRINK BEFORE WE GO OUT...

RS; BY MAGIC I UPSET THE CALM SEA CALM THE STORMY ON

ANIMATE AND MOVE THE STONES AS IF THEY WERE AL

PPRUMMMBLE

...AND RISE AGAIN,
ARCADIA!

WROOOOOUUS...

AAH!

UGH!

SQUEAK
SQUEAK

WHAT'S GOING ON OUT THERE, GIRLS?

IF IT'S SOME TYPE OF *PRIDE FLASH MOB*...I'M READY!

Queer Witches

"IT LOOKS LIKE THE *STREET'S* BECOME A *CANYON*... HOW MANY *BUILDINGS* EVEN SURVIVED THIS...*THING?*

"...AND HOW MANY *PEOPLE?* WHAT *HAPPENED* TO THE PEOPLE ON THE *STREET?*

"...WHAT ABOUT THE PEOPLE *INSIDE* ALL THE *BUILDINGS?*

"WE NEED TO KNOW WHAT'S *HAPPENING* OUT THERE... HOW TO *PROTECT* OURSELVES...AND WHERE TO *HIDE.*

"IT *COULDN'T* HAVE BEEN A NATURAL DISASTER, NOT THIS...THIS ISN'T ANY *NATURE* WE KNOW OF.

"IT'S SOMETHING *DIFFERENT*...JUST LIKE THE NIGHT *BECKY* CAME INTO OUR LIVES."

WHAT THE FUCK...

WAIT... YOU SEE IT TOO?!

EVERYONE INSIDE... NOW!

Chapter 12

Chapter 13

DARKFORT, THE ROYAL PALACE.

ARCADIA...

EVERYTHING IS NOW *FINALLY* AS IT WAS *THEN!*

THE *TIME OF STORIES* HAS RETURNED!

...SADLY, THEY *NEVER* WILL, DEVERA. I AM DESTINED TO WALK WITH THEM FOREVER.

YOUR *MAJESTY*... YOU SHOULD LIE DOWN. THE WOUNDS INFLICTED BY THE WITCH'S *CURSE* HAVE YET TO FULLY HEAL...

REMAIN WITH MY COURTIERS, DESTROY EVERY CRYSTAL YOU FIND, SO THAT NO ONE MAY AGAIN WEAR SOME ILLUSORY SHADE IN OUR MIDST.

WE MUST ENSURE THAT THAT SECRET IS NEVER MENTIONED AGAIN.

"KING TARANIS... WITH THE *RIGHT* SACRIFICE, *I* COULD POTENTIALLY HEAL YOUR WOUNDS..."

"THE *HEART OF ARCADIA* SHOWS ME YOUR RITUAL'S EVERY *IMPERFECTION.*"

"I'VE HAD MORE THAN ENOUGH OF YOUR MAGIC, MEDEA."

"A RITUAL THAT REQUIRES *TIME!* I *FLOODED* THE SUBWAY TUNNELS WITH POWER, THEREBY CREATING A NEW CIRCULATORY SYSTEM OF *LEY LINES...*"

"*INCOMPLETE.* DON'T PRETEND YOU'RE UNAWARE. THERE ARE PLACES THAT YET *RESIST* YOUR MAGIC..."

"EVEN *NOW,* ARCADIA IS--"

"...STORY *TEMPLES,* BOOKSTORES AND LIBRARIES, SCHOOLS, MUSEUMS AND EVEN... *COMIC SHOPS...* THAT *SURVIVE* IN SPITE OF THE *TRANSFORMATION.*"

"DO NOT *SHOW* YOURSELF AGAIN UNTIL THE SITUATION IS *RESOLVED.*"

"*ONLY* THEN WILL MY *DREAM* BE COMPLETE."

"AS...YOU *COMMAND,* YOUR MAJESTY."

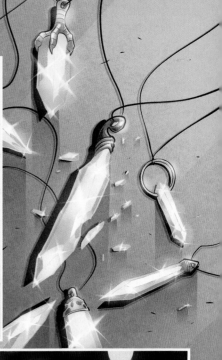

CR1CK

NOW *NO ONE* HAS TO *HIDE.*

YOU... YOU ARE MEDEA'S *PUPPY,* ARE YOU NOT? THE *RENAMED WARLOCK.*

SHE PROMISED ME YOU'D BE *KEPT* ON A LEASH...

OWAIN, YOUR MAJESTY... AND I *LIVE* TO SERVE YOU.

AH! SO IT'S NOT JUST *HER* THAT HOLDS YOUR *LOYALTY...*

MY *ENTIRE* EXISTENCE IS A COMPLETE ACT OF *SUBMISSION,* YOUR MAJESTY.

SHE'S *BOUND* A *WITCH...*WHAT SWEET IRONY-- *NGHH∃∃*

YOUR MAJESTY! I CAN...

NO! NO MORE WITCHCRAFT!

OUT OF MY WAY.

OUR *HOME* ON *IOS* WAS LEFT TOTALLY *EMPTY*. YOU USED UP *ALL* OF OUR MAGIC RESERVES.

I *KNOW* YOU TOOK ALL OF IT TO *HOMER'S TOMB* BEFORE YOU LEFT...

...AND *NOW* I *ALSO* KNOW WHAT YOU WERE HIDING BEHIND YOUR SILENCE. *YOU HAVE THE POWER TO CHANGE WORLDS, MAYBE EVEN CREATE NEW ONES.*

YOU ARE GREATER THAN HIM.

HE *MAY* HOLD THE HEART OF ARCADIA IN HIS CHEST; *BUT YOU* HAVE A POWER FAR MORE ANCIENT; ONE THAT TOWERS ABOVE HIS OWN.

I HAVE NO *CHOICE* BUT TO *FOLLOW* HIS ORDERS FOR NOW.

THAT IS *WHY* I MUST GO ABOUT THIS *THE HARD WAY.*

I KNOW I PROMISED NOT TO *WEAR* IT, BUT...

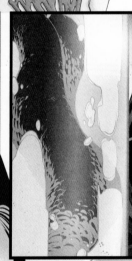

NO! NOT *THAT!* THAT'S... *PLEASE!* NO!

YES. REDUCED, ENCHANTED AND PRESERVED. BUT IT IS *STILL EXACTLY* WHAT IT *APPEARS* TO BE.

NOW... MAKE ROOM.

Chapter 14

YOU CAN'T STAND THERE DAZED, LOVE. WE HAVE TO GO...

...AND IF ANYONE TRIES TO STOP US, WE LET LOOSE A SECOND STONEWALL ON THEM.

THERE'S NO POINT IN WALLING OURSELVES OFF IN HERE FOREVER.

ONE OF US WILL STAY BEHIND ON GUARD, BUT WE'VE GOT TO FIND *BECKY.*

IT'S...IT'S *TOO* DANGEROUS...

MAYBE IT IS... BUT WE'VE ALL GOT SOMEONE TO LOOK FOR, HERE. WE'LL FIND THE SURVIVORS, THEN WE'LL FIGURE OUT HOW TO GET OUT OF THIS NIGHTMARE... *TOGETHER.*

WHAT A FUCKING MESS... BUT WHATEVER. OKAY...

FIRST I WILL SAVE EVERYONE AND THEN I WILL HUNT DOWN TARANIS.

WHAT HAPPENED TO FER AND LADY MACBETH...?

BEEP

IF WE ALL ENDED UP IN THIS FANTASY WORLD, THEN THE DRUID AND THE OLD HAG HAVE TO BE HERE SOMEWHERE.

I NEED TO FIND THEM, AND IN THE MEANTIME, I'LL GET INTO SOMETHING MORE FUNCTIONAL.

BUT THEY ARE, I MEAN...LADY MACBETH TRULY IS MISSING, I DO NOT FEEL HER HERE IN ARCADIA...

FZZT

...AND AS FOR FER, YOU SAW HIM...TARANIS, HE...I MEAN, FER IS--

DON'T EVEN FUCKING SAY IT.

FER IS STILL ALIVE.

I CHANGED HIS NAME. I'LL FIND A WAY TO INVOKE HIM AGAIN.

YOU DON'T UNDERSTAND, FER...

WHAT? WHAT ARE YOU...LOOKING AT...?

DARKFORT, THE GALLERY OF A HUNDRED CROSSROADS.

Chapter 15

ARCADIA, ROCK OF THE THREE SUNS.

TWO YEARS LATER.

THE *WAR* WAS NOT LONG IN COMING AND SOON OVERWHELMED EVERY REALM.

LOSSES WERE *INCALCULABLE,* ON EVERY FRONT.

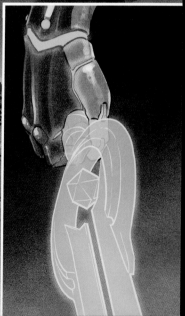

THE WITCH GATHERED THE SURVIVING HUMANS AND *DISSIDENT STORIES,* SETTING UP AN OUTPOST WHERE ARCADIAN MAGIC WAS BANISHED.

Epilogue

IT'LL BE *YOU* WHO MEETS THE ONE WITH THE LAST HEART, THE ONE THAT SERVES THE KING.

THREE WOMEN MET YEARS AGO. AFTER THAT MEETING, TWO OF THEM BECAME MOTHERS...

THIS DAUGHTER OF THEIRS HAD A *PRODIGIOUS* HEART...

...THE HEART OF A HERO.

WE HAVE TO GET YOU OUT OF HERE AS SOON AS POSSIBLE... TELL ME HOW YOU FEEL...

I'M JUST A LITTLE CONFUSED. THE TRUCK WAS COMING TOWARDS US, WE TRIED TO STEER AWAY BUT THERE WAS SOMETHING IN THE SKY...

SOMETHING *HUGE*...AND DANGEROUS. IT WAS BIGGER THAN AN EAGLE...WE'RE STILL IN DANGER, I THINK...

YOU WILL BE A GOOD MOTHER...

FLAP

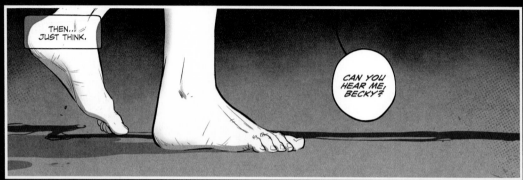

SPLASH

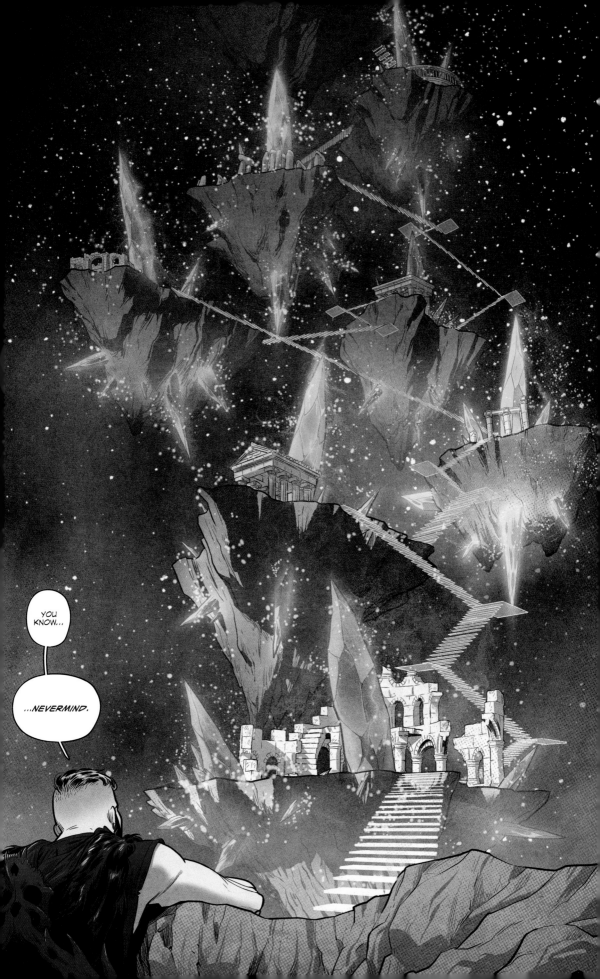

DEIMNE...

FIONN MAC CUMHAILL, DRUID. THAT'S HOW I'LL BE REMEMBERED... YOU *KNOW* THAT.

OF COURSE. AND YOU'RE A *JERK AS USUAL*. WHAT ARE YOU DOING HERE?

WAITING. I'M *WAITING* TO HEAR THE PEOPLE COMING FROM THE *STAIRS OF PURE FORMS*, I'VE BEEN DEAD FOR HUNDREDS OF YEARS ALREADY.

IRON? OR...?

WITCHES. IN THE END, THEY TOOK THEIR REVENGE. NO MORE *RESURRECTIONS*, THEY *BANNED* ME. DO THEY STILL *EXIST* IN YOUR TIME?

FEW DO.

ANYWAY, I DIDN'T WANT TO CROSS THE THRESHOLD ALONE... SHALL WE GO, TOGETHER?

JUST LET ME *UNDERSTAND* FOR A MOMENT... WERE *YOU*... WAITING FOR *ME*?

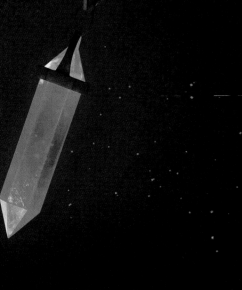

NO MORE SECRETS

or *How Stories Already Won the War Against Reality*

An afterwor(l)d by Marco B Bucci

If you just finished reading this volume, and I guess you have since this is an afterword, after all, you know there's a specific moment in this story arc in which the Secret, the powerful enchantment that kept Stories close, but hidden from our sight, gets shattered. The fact that Manhattan becomes Arcadia, the realm of Stories, might have something to do with it, but we'll get there.

So, we are now all in Arcadia, along with Becky, her friends, and her enemies. We must forget the "real" world in which we were gray and devoid of magic to embrace this new fantasy place, dangerous but also full of adventures and revelations.

There is only one limit to the strength of the ritual with which Medea transformed Manhattan into Arcadia: **the temples of stories.** In bookstores, libraries, comic shops, private collections, and shops that store books, the Naming ritual did not take effect. The love, dedication, and veneration men have for literary works have shielded these places from the powerful transformation. They are intact, as are all who were inside them.

I have never doubted that there is magic in such places and that they must be preserved, visited, and supported. The places where we meet, discover new stories, meet characters we are connected to, or talk to other readers who share a passion for imaginary worlds are sacred. Within them we travel in time, backward in our personal history, distinctly remembering

ourselves, who fell in love several times. The strength of Narration is the only one that can oppose that of True Names.

After all, they are two forms of magic that speak the same language.

But more importantly, let's face it: you just read an ending that's not really an ending. Surely it will not have made you breathe that sigh of relief that is usually sought in the last pages of a series. In these last chapters nothing is given away, the plot armors fall apart, and all hope seems lost.

Patrick was not saved.
Lady Macbeth is still trapped in her story.
~~**Fer Doirich is dead.**~~ **(wink, wink)**
Sophie was killed.
Becky has found herself, but not her heart.
Taranis won, but will suffer forever.

Defeating Medea didn't give Becky the chance to settle the unfinished business he had with the king, her true opponent. There was no revenge, just fury and magic mixed together. Victory over the dragon will not bring the dead back to life, it will not give peace to anyone. Overwhelmed by power, she has decided to defeat Medea by becoming the villain of this story. **So who is the Hero? Is there anyone really innocent in the NOMEN OMEN saga?**

The answer is simple: I personally don't believe in innocent people, but most of all, I don't believe in simple people. Darkness, anger, fallacy, and weakness belong to everyone to varying degrees. That's why Becky isn't a real hero. I never wanted her to be a hero. I have always dreamed of her as a real person, capable of making mistakes even when history dictates that we do the right thing. We saw her opportunity to be better than her tormentors. It was

her time to become, without a doubt, the heroine...yet she failed.

In life, it goes like this: sometimes the wrong thing is done and the value of each of us is not measured by our mistakes, but by the ability to understand them, accept them, and remedy them.

That's why ARCADIA exists! With the change of the True Name of Manhattan the series needed to change names too. We've had this metamorphosis in mind since the beginning and the time for it has finally come. In this second macro-arc of the saga, we'll follow the life of Becky and Taranis several years after the ending you have just read. A bloody war continues to plague the fantasy world created by Medea's ritual. Becky rules a portion of the surviving human beings while Taranis protects the Incarnate Stories he has sheltered from her fury. Will Becky be able to bring Manhattan back to our reality? Will she finally recover her heart? How far will the conflict go?

Jacopo and I can't wait to embark on this new journey with you that from urban fantasy officially turns into fantasy... urban! ARCADIA Volume I - Mad World was released in Italy in autumn 2020 and at the time of printing this trade, we don't know how and when Arcadia will arrive in the USA. **But it certainly will!**

Now...before I let go of the credits, I would like to spend my last words to thank you who are reading. You have come this far, and this is a magical act, part of a ritual that we shared together and that we hope you will want to conclude with us in Arcadia.

MBB

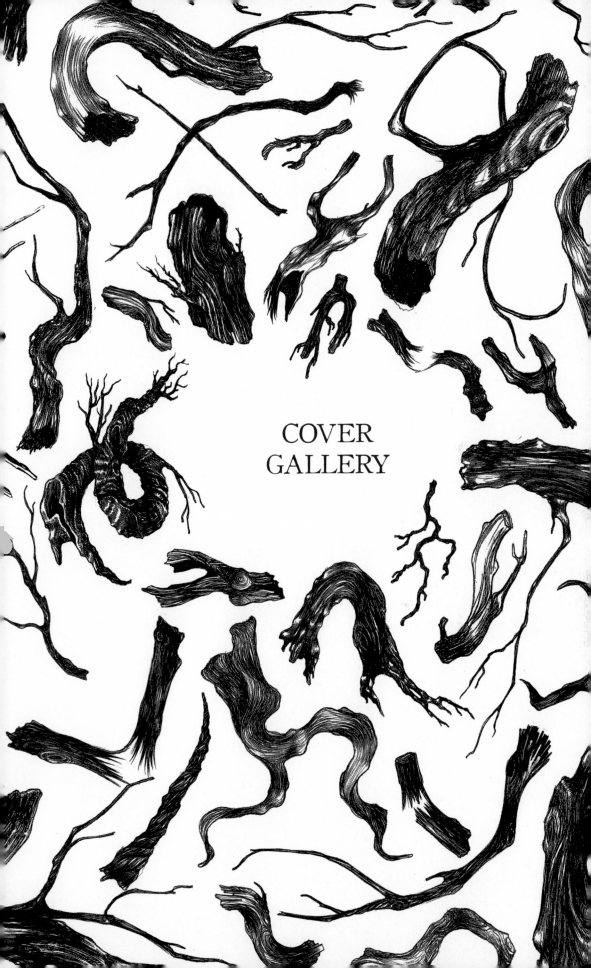

COVER
GALLERY

Issue 9 Variant by KRIS ANKA

Issue 11 Variant by MIRKA ANDOLFO

Issue 13 Variant by WERTHER DELL'EDERA

Issue 15 Variant by PEPE LARRAZ

Pin-up by JACOPO CAMAGNI

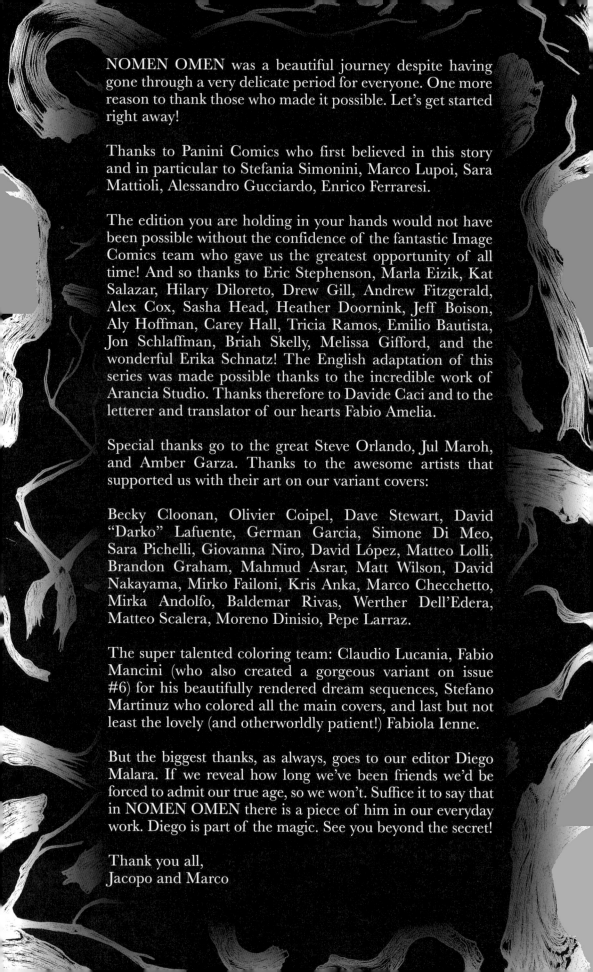

NOMEN OMEN was a beautiful journey despite having gone through a very delicate period for everyone. One more reason to thank those who made it possible. Let's get started right away!

Thanks to Panini Comics who first believed in this story and in particular to Stefania Simonini, Marco Lupoi, Sara Mattioli, Alessandro Gucciardo, Enrico Ferraresi.

The edition you are holding in your hands would not have been possible without the confidence of the fantastic Image Comics team who gave us the greatest opportunity of all time! And so thanks to Eric Stephenson, Marla Eizik, Kat Salazar, Hilary Diloreto, Drew Gill, Andrew Fitzgerald, Alex Cox, Sasha Head, Heather Doornink, Jeff Boison, Aly Hoffman, Carey Hall, Tricia Ramos, Emilio Bautista, Jon Schlaffman, Briah Skelly, Melissa Gifford, and the wonderful Erika Schnatz! The English adaptation of this series was made possible thanks to the incredible work of Arancia Studio. Thanks therefore to Davide Caci and to the letterer and translator of our hearts Fabio Amelia.

Special thanks go to the great Steve Orlando, Jul Maroh, and Amber Garza. Thanks to the awesome artists that supported us with their art on our variant covers:

Becky Cloonan, Olivier Coipel, Dave Stewart, David "Darko" Lafuente, German Garcia, Simone Di Meo, Sara Pichelli, Giovanna Niro, David López, Matteo Lolli, Brandon Graham, Mahmud Asrar, Matt Wilson, David Nakayama, Mirko Failoni, Kris Anka, Marco Checchetto, Mirka Andolfo, Baldemar Rivas, Werther Dell'Edera, Matteo Scalera, Moreno Dinisio, Pepe Larraz.

The super talented coloring team: Claudio Lucania, Fabio Mancini (who also created a gorgeous variant on issue #6) for his beautifully rendered dream sequences, Stefano Martinuz who colored all the main covers, and last but not least the lovely (and otherworldly patient!) Fabiola Ienne.

But the biggest thanks, as always, goes to our editor Diego Malara. If we reveal how long we've been friends we'd be forced to admit our true age, so we won't. Suffice it to say that in NOMEN OMEN there is a piece of him in our everyday work. Diego is part of the magic. See you beyond the secret!

Thank you all,
Jacopo and Marco

WHOEVER YOU ARE,
WHOEVER YOU WANT TO BE,
ADVENTURE AWAITS

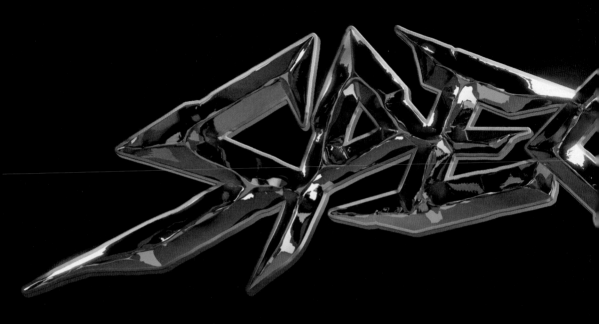

THE URBAN FANTASY
TABLETOP ROLEPLAYING GAME FOR **5**E,
SET IN THE **NOMEN OMEN** UNIVERSE

MANA PROJECT
STUDIO

5E

BIOS

Jacopo Camagni has been working in the comics and illustration industry for over twenty years. In 1998, he drew an original graphic novel dedicated to *Lupin the 3rd* under the supervision of the late Monkey Punch, creator of the character. Ten years later, he began working for Marvel Comics. Since then he's lent his art to some of the most famous characters of the Marvel Universe, such as Longshot, Hawkeye, Deadpool, Deadpool the Duck, the X-Men and Kanan from the *Star Wars* franchise.

Marco B. Bucci, born in 1981, represents a new breed of storyteller. Photographer, designer, illustrator and writer, in 2004 he founded Studio Dronio with Jacopo Camagni, with whom he created *Magna Veritas*, a comic book series published by Soleil in France in 2005. He also wrote the backstory of *Dogs of War*, a CMON Ltd boardgame, and co-created the tabletop RPG *Memento Mori*. In 2018 he co-wrote *Codex Gigas*, a *Memento Mori* companion book that serves as a full-fledged grimoire as well. Today, he juggles his work as a photographer for prestigious fashion labels with his artistic role in the production of role-playing game manuals, and with his work writing comics and novels.